Presented to

_____

Presented by

_____

Date

Lady Ademola (1913 - 2002)

Lady Kofoworola Aina ADEMOLA was born on 21 May 1913, daughter of the Honorable Eric Moore, an eminent lawyer and member of the Colonial Legislative Council. Her mother was Arabella Moore (nee Vaughan) of the respected Vaughan family with strong roots in the Southern states of America.

In 1935, Lady Ademola became the first Nigerian, indeed, the first known black African woman, to graduate from Oxford University. She married Adetokunbo Ademola, son of Sir Oladapo Ademola, the Alake of Egbaland on 31 January 1939. Lady Ademola with her husband, were knighted by the Queen of England in 1956. As the first national president of the National Council for Women's Societies, she stood shoulder to shoulder with other eminent Nigerian women to fight for the betterment of womanhood. She was honoured with the medal of the Officer of the Federal Republic (OFR), of the Federal Republic of Nigeria by the government of Sir Abubakar Tafawa Balewa.

Later in life, she took to writing African folk tales - the "Lady K" books - and working on the compilation of African Proverbs which has proved quite popular. A prolific letter writer and an excellent public speaker, she was honoured by the Association of Nigerian Authors. She died on the 15th of May 2002 at the age of 89.

AFRICAN PROVERBS II

Compiled By
LADY ADEMOLA

An imprint of
BOOKCRAFT

An imprint of

BOOKCRAFT

23, Adebajo Street, Kongi Layout,
New Bodija
P.O. Box 16279, Ibadan, Nigeria.
Tel/Fax: +234 -2- 810 3238; 751 7153
Mobile: +234 -803 344 7889, 803 722 0773, 807 319 9967
E-mail: olayebi@yahoo.com; info@bookcraftafrica.com;
editor@bookcraftafrica.com
Website: www.bookcraftafrica.com

ISBN 978-8135-61-7

CONTENTS

CONTENTS

I t is now exactly ten years since the first edition of this handy and attractive volume – containing timeless Gems of African culture – was initially published.

African proverbs – whether pithy and sometimes inscrutable words of wisdom, or simple, everyday truisms – have over the ages, been used to warn, to instruct or to admonish.

Taken from countries and cultures across Africa, the proverbs in this volume reflect the beliefs, cultural values and the heritage of the peoples of the continent – the Ashanti, the Wolof, the Yoruba, the Zulu, the Hutu, the Kikuyu, among so many others.

The attractive layout and design, and the handy format in which it is presented, make this book, as always, a timeless and useful gift for all seasons.

"Owe ni esin oro...

(Proverbs are the vehicle for conveying the hidden essence of words)

Proverbs enrich a language: they give in-depth meaning to words.

So goes the Yoruba saying. Indeed in bygone days among the Yoruba speaking people of Nigeria, a person who could intersperse speech with apt proverbs was regarded as someone with great wisdom and culture. He was highly respected, for to the Yorubas, proverbs contain some philosophy as well as moral and cultural tenets.

This conception of the value of proverbs in the enrichment of language was, however, by no means limited to the Yoruba ethnic group. These proverbs submitted to the BBC African Service were contributed by listeners from several Sub-Saharan countries, albeit and, understandably so, the majority of them originated from the Anglophone areas.

The usage of proverbs as "words of wisdom" is universal and the great number subscribed to the BBC African Service confirms that

9

African nations very much regard them and employ them as such. In this compilation, it will be noticed that there are striking similarities of thought and ideas, phrased in almost identical words, in some of the proverbs contributed from countries as far apart as those of East and West Africa. A Malawi proverb says: "a child on its mother's back does not know the distance covered." It's Nigerian counterpart states: "a baby on its mother's back does not know that its destination is far." A proverb from Swaziland which says: "if you follow an elephant, your feet will not get drenched with dew" almost synonymous with the one from Ghana that states: "if you walk behind an elephant, you will not get drenched with dew."

There are also some proverbs that convey the same precepts that are expressed in different words. A proverb from Sudan says: "the first camel pulls the caravan, but it is the last one that gets the beating" while "the cow at the end of the herd receives the strokes" is recorded from Ghana.

In the process of translating the proverbs from their original African languages into English, some may have lost their authenticity and may fail to make the impact originally intended. Two proverbs, the meaning of which are somewhat puzzling serve as examples. "Salt does not praise itself", says a Ghanaian proverb. "If a man has only one coin in his pocket it does not make much noise", says the other from Burundi. What do they mean? (the Burundi proverbs was later interpreted to the BBC commentator as meaning "if a man has only one wife, he would not have as much trouble as he would if he had more than one"). In this collection, however, the number of proverbs affected adversely by translation is minimal; the majority retain their true African flavour and remain as they ever were. Some thousands of African proverbs have been submitted for broadcast and the ones in this collection are but an insignificant few.

Nevertheless, it is my hope that they will give credence to their usage as words of wisdom. and to their enrichment of African languages. Above all, I hope that they will be as much appreciated and enjoyed as they have been by me in compiling them.

LADY ADEMOLA
Lagos, Nigeria
September, 2000

EVEN WHEN THE BIRD IS UP IN THE SKY, ITS MIND IS ALWAYS ON THE GROUND.

WHEN A HUNTER SETS
A TRAP USING A GOAT AS
BAIT, HE DOES NOT EXPECT
TO CATCH A RABBIT.
Nigeria

THE HEN THAT PECKS ON
A ROCK MUST TRUST THE
STRENGTH OF ITS BEAK.
Uganda

A BIG PLATE DOES NOT CONSUME A LITTLE FOOD.

Zambia

AMBITION WITHOUT
KNOWLEDGE IS LIKE A BOAT
ON DRY LAND.
Ghana

FINE TREES BEAR JUICY FRUITS.

Botswana

NO MATTER HOW GOOD A DOG'S SUPPER IS, IT WILL STILL EAT GARBAGE.
Cote D'Ivoire

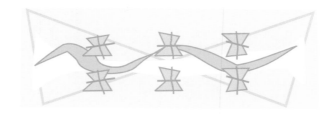

KOKODUS MEET KOKODUS AT THE FUNERAL OF A KOKODU; MEANING BIRDS OF A FEATHER FLOCK TOGETHER.
Cote D'Ivoire

IF A MAN IS BORN IN A STABLE,
HE DOES NOT BECOME A
HORSE, BUT IF HE LIVES LONG
IN THE STABLE, HE WILL
BEHAVE LIKE
A HORSE.
Ethiopia

IT IS OVER
HONEY THAT THE HONEYBEE
BECOMES AGGRESSIVE.
Guinea

A BEE CAN NEVER BE AS
SWEET AS HONEY NO
MATTER HOW LONG IT STAYS
IN THE BEEHIVE.

Gambia

A DONKEY CANNOT
GET RID OF ITS
LARGE EARS
MERELY
BY SHAKING ITS
HEAD VIGOROUSLY.

Gambia

FINE COWS GIVE GOOD MILK.
Ghana

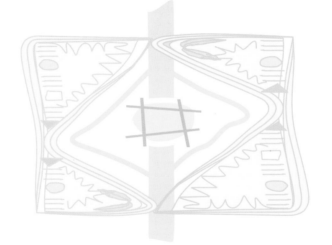

A HEN CAN NEVER LAY DUCK
EGGS.
Nigeria

A CHILD WHO IS NOT TAUGHT WELL AT HOME BY HIS MOTHER WILL BE TAUGHT BADLY IN THE OUTSIDE WORLD.

Guinea

A CHAMELEON MAY CHANGE ITS COLOUR BUT IT DOES NOT CHANGE ITS NATURE.

Kenya

THE SIZE OF A CHICKEN DOES
NOT LIE IN ITS FEATHERS.
South Africa

THE WAY A CAT WALKS IS NOT
THE WAY IT CATCHES RATS.
South Africa

THE MORE FEATHERS A
CHICKEN HAS, THE BIGGER IT
LOOKS.
Zambia

NO MATTER HOW DARK IT IS,
THE COCK WILL ALWAYS
KNOW WHEN TO CROW AT
DAWN.

Swaziland

HE WHO WOULD BE A LIAR
MUST HAVE A GOOD MEMORY.
Uganda

IT IS A PATIENT HORSE THAT
DOES NOT STUMBLE, AND A
PATIENT WIFE WHO DOES
NOT GRUMBLE.
Uganda

TO LEARN TO FLY, A BIRD
MUST FIRST LEARN TO LEAVE
THE NEST.

IT IS A FOOLISH COCK THAT CROWS AT DUSK.

Zimbabwe

A FROG NEVER JUMPS BACKWARDS.

Zimbabwe

26

NOT ALL THE TREES IN THE FOREST MAKE GOOD FIREWOOD.
Sudan

MILK IS EXACTLY THE SAME WHETHER IT COMES FROM A BLACK COW OR A WHITE ONE.
Tanzania

A DISEASE THAT
WOULD KILL A
DOG FIRST
TAKES AWAY
ITS SENSE OF
SMELL

Lesotho

A STONE THROWN IN RAGE SELDOM HITS ITS TARGET.
Malawi

DO NOT SWIM IN SHALLOW WATERS IF YOU DO NOT WANT YOUR BACK TO SHOW.
Malawi

A HEN THAT SWALLOWS A NEEDLE WILL NOT LIVE LONG ENOUGH TO PREEN ITSELF.
Cameroon

29

IF YOUR FOOT SLIPS, YOU CAN
RECOVER YOUR BALANCE, IF YOUR
TONGUE SLIPS, YOU CANNOT
RECOVER YOUR WORDS.
Ghana

IF YOU DO NOT BRING FIRE NEAR A
TORTOISE, IT WILL NOT STICK OUT ITS
HEAD.
Ghana

WHEN THE GODS WANT A DOG TO
DIE, THEY SIMPLY NUMB HIS SENSE OF
SMELL.
Uganda

WHEN YOU BRING INSECT-INFESTED
WOOD INTO YOUR HOUSE, YOU
INVITE LIZARDS IN AS WELL.
Cape Verde

TO RUN AWAY FROM THE STINGS
OF THE HONEYBEES, YOU MUST
ABANDON THE HONEY.
Cameroon

DO NOT DIG A HOLE
FOR YOUR ENEMY, FOR
YOU DO NOT KNOW WHO
MAY FALL INSIDE IT.
Ethiopia

THOSE WHO REFUSE TO DRINK FROM
THE WELL OF KNOWLEDGE WILL DIE OF
THIRST IN THE DESERT OF IGNORANCE.
Guinea

32

THE SPOKEN WORD IS LIKE A STONE,
ONCE IT IS THROWN, IT CANNOT BE
RETRIEVED.
Ghana

YOU DO NOT KILL A CALF IN FRONT OF
ITS MOTHER.
Kenya

HE WHO REFUSES TO OBEY CANNOT
COMMAND.
Kenya

WHEN TWO BULLS FIGHT, IT IS THE
GRASS THAT SUFFERS.
Kenya

THE HIGHER THE MONKEY CLIMBS, THE
MORE ITS BUTTOCKS ARE EXPOSED.
Malawi

WHEN THE SEA DRIES UP, THE SUN
SHOULD SHARE IN ITS SHAME.
Ghana

IF A CHILD EATS SOUR FRUIT, IT IS THE FATHER'S TEETH THAT ARE SET ON EDGE.

Malawi

HE WHO WISHES TO PICK STONES FROM THE BOTTOM OF A RIVER MUST BE PREPARED TO GET WET.

Nigeria

AN ANIMAL THAT EATS THORNS MUST
KNOW HOW TO DIGEST THEM IN ITS
STOMACH.

Nigeria

IF YOU WISH TO GATHER HONEY, YOU
MUST BE PREPARED TO RISK THE
PAINFUL STINGS OF THE BEES.

Nigeria

HE WHO VOLUNTEERS HIS HEAD FOR
THE BREAKING OF A COCONUT SHOULD
NOT EXPECT TO EAT FROM IT.

Nigeria

36

HE WHO SELLS SAND AS SALT IS PAID
STONES AS MONEY.
Nigeria

HE WHO SETS FIRE TO HIS FATHER'S
HOUSE WILL INHERIT THE WRECKAGE.
Nigeria

IT IS ONLY WHEN AN EGG BREAKS THAT
YOU REALIZE THAT IT IS NOT ALL WHITE.
Sierra Leone

CHICKENS THAT CACKLE
TOO LOUDLY WILL NOT
HEAR THE HAWK COMING.
Sudan

THOSE WHO SOW
THORNS SHOULD NOT
EXPECT TO REAP FLOWERS.
Swaziland

IF YOU ARE HUNTING A MAN-EATING
ANIMAL, BE PREPARED BECAUSE YOU
ARE BEING HUNTED YOURSELF.
Uganda

A TOAD WILL REALIZE THE IMPORTANCE
OF WATER ONLY WHEN THE POND GETS
DRY.
Zambia

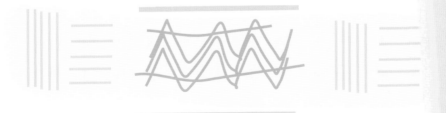

A MAN WHO IS ACCUSED OF STEALING GOATS SHOULD NOT ENTERTAIN HIS GUEST WITH DRIED MEAT.
TOGO

YOU CANNOT STRETCH YOUR HANDS FURTHER THAN THE BONES IN THEM WILL ALLOW.

Cameroon

A TORTOISE
FOR LACK
OF VANITY
CARRIES ITS
SHELL
WHEREVER
IT GOES.
Zambia

THE ANTELOPE SAYS
THAT HE IS NEVER
ANGRY WITH THE
HUNTER WHO SHOT AT
HIM, BUT WITH THE DOG
THAT DROVE HIM FROM
HIS HIDING PLACE.

Lesotho

THE PALM-WINE TAPPER IS LIKE A KING
TO A DRUNKARD.
Cameroon

A COCONUT SHELL FULL OF WATER IS
LIKE AN OCEAN TO A SMALL ANT.
Nigeria

IF A DOG CHASES A LIZARD IN THE RAIN,
HE SHOULD UNDERSTAND THAT HIS
COAT WILL REMAIN WET LONG AFTER
THE LIZARD IS DRY.
Namibia

A TEAM OF PIGS LED BY A LION IS MORE
FORMIDABLE THAN A TEAM OF LIONS LED
BY A PIG.
Gambia

A DAY OF PEACE IN TIMES OF STRESS IS
LIKE A THOUSAND DAYS IN PARADISE.
Nigeria

ONLY WHEN THE CAT IS DEAD CAN THE MOUSE LICK ITS NOSE.
Zimbabwe

IF THE FLY SITTING ON TOP OF A PALM-WINE CALABASH SAYS IT IS DRUNK, WHAT WILL THE FLY INSIDE THE CALABASH SAY.
Nigeria

EVEN AMONG ANTS, THERE ARE GIANTS.
Nigeria

A WOMAN WORRIES ABOUT THE FUTURE UNTIL SHE GETS A HUSBAND; A MAN NEVER WORRIES ABOUT THE FUTURE UNTIL HE GETS A WIFE.
Uganda

WHEN A JACKAL
WANTS TO CATCH
A SHEEP, IT
DRESSES UP IN A
LAMB'S SKIN.
Lesotho

THE CAT WILL HIDE ITS CLAWS UNDER ITS PAWS IN ORDER TO FEIGN FRIENDSHIP WITH THE RAT.
Uganda

A SET OF WHITE TEETH DOES NOT INDICATE A PURE HEART.
Nigeria

IF YOU WANT TO BURN DOWN YOUR HOUSE, YOUR ENEMY WILL LEND YOU A MATCH.
Zimbabwe

WHEN A CHILD'S GROUNDNUT IS BURNT IN THE FIRE, HE EATS THE NEXT ONE RAW.

Uganda

YOU DO NOT CONSULT AN ORACLE
WHEN YOU ALREADY KNOW THE CAUSE
OF YOUR ILLNESS.
Cameroon

A BABE IN ITS MOTHER'S WOMB DOES
NOT FEEL THE SMOKE IN ITS MOTHER'S
KITCHEN.
Cameroon

NEW BROOMS SWEEP CLEAN, BUT IT IS
THE OLD ONE THAT KNOWS ALL THE
DIRTY CORNERS.
Ghana

YOU DON'T TOUCH WHAT YOU CANNOT SEE.
Kenya

IF YOU KNOW ONLY ONE TUNE YOU CANNOT DANCE ALL NIGHT.
Malawi

HE WHO SPLITS HIS OWN FIREWOOD WARMS HIMSELF TWICE.
Malawi

IF YOU ARE TALLER THAN YOUR FATHER, THAT DOES NOT MAKE YOU HIS PEER.
Malawi

HE WHO HAS NOT TASTED WHAT IS BITTER WILL NEVER KNOW THAT WHICH IS SWEET.
Sierra Leone

NO MATTER HOW LONG THE BEARD GROWS, IT CANNOT COMPARE ITSELF IN AGE WITH THE EYEBROW.
South Africa

HE WHO SLEEPS ON A MAT KNOWS THE
TYPE OF BUG THAT BITES HIM.
Tanzania

IT IS BETTER TO LIVE IN THE CORNER OF
A ROOF THAN TO SHARE A LARGER
ROOM WITH A QUARRELSOME WIFE.
Uganda

THE EYES OF OUR ELDERS DO NOT SHED
TEARS FOR NO REASON.
Uganda

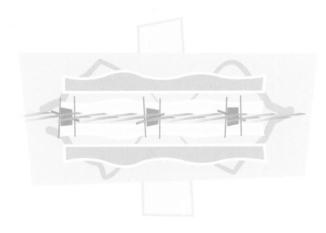

AN OLD MAN'S MOUTH MAY BE TWISTED,
BUT HIS WORDS ARE NOT...
Zambia

FORESIGHT

NEVER FIGHT A
STRANGER IN THE
DARK, HE MAY
TURN OUT TO BE
YOUR BROTHER.
Zambia

56

CROPS THAT ARE PLANTED ON A
HILLTOP WILL BE HARVESTED BY THE
WIND.
Cameroon

BEFORE YOU CUT DOWN YOUR
COCONUT TREE, CAREFULLY MEASURE
THE DISTANCE BETWEEN YOUR
NEIGHBOUR'S HOUSE AND THE TREE.
Cameroon

TAKE CARE NOT TO LOSE WHAT YOU
ARE HOLDING UNDER YOUR ARMPIT
WHEN TRYING TO HOLD ON TO THE
LOAD ON YOUR HEAD.
Ethiopia

A MAN WITH ONLY ONE ARROW TO HIS
BOW SHOULD NOT SHOOT IT FAR FROM
HOME.
Ghana

IF YOU LISTEN TO THE VOICE OF THUNDER
YOU WILL NOT BE SOAKED WITH RAIN.
Ghana

A PERSON WHO HAS NOT SECURED A
SPACE ON THE FLOOR SHOULD NOT LOOK
FOR A MAT TO SPREAD.
Kenya

IF SOMEONE INTENDS TO ROAST YOU, YOU DO NOT SMEAR YOURSELF WITH OIL AND SIT BY THE FIRESIDE AWAITING HIM.

Nigeria

A GIRL WHO GOES TO THE STREAM EARLY IN THE MORNING FETCHES CLEAN WATER.

Nigeria

A BEAUTIFUL PARROT THAT KNOWS ITS FEATHERS ARE IN HIGH DEMAND SHOULD NOT BUILD ITS NEST CLOSE TO THE GROUND.

Nigeria

IF YOU SAY YOU WILL BREAK THE SKY
WHEN YOUR FATHER DIES, STARTING
CRACKING IT WHILE HE IS STILL ALIVE.
Sierra Leone

HE WHO SHOOTS AN ARROW
UPWARDS TO THE SKY SHOULD HAVE
HIS HEAD PROTECTED.
Sudan

A MAN WHO SITS BY THE BEACH WHERE FISHERMAN MAKE THEIR CATCH WILL NEVER EAT PLAIN RICE.

Zambia

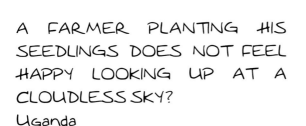

A FARMER PLANTING HIS SEEDLINGS DOES NOT FEEL HAPPY LOOKING UP AT A CLOUDLESS SKY?

Uganda

A SMILE IS THE STRONGEST WEAPON IN THE BATTLE OF LIFE.
Ghana

KIND WORDS DO NOT WEAR OUT THE TONGUE.
Liberia

THE ONLY THING TO DO WITH GOOD ADVICE IS TO PASS IT ON.
Uganda

IF A CHICKEN DOES
NOT DIG, IT DOES
NOTFEED.

Cameroon

IT IS NOT NECESSARY FOR FINGERS TO LOOK ALIKE, BUT IS NECESSARY FOR THEM TO CO-OPERATE.

Kenya

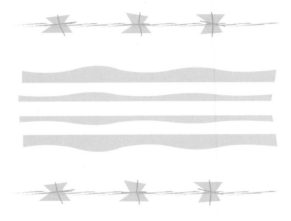

YOU GAIN INTEREST ONLY ON WHAT YOU INVEST.

Lesotho

WATER FLOWING IN A RIVER DOES
NOT WAIT FOR A THIRSTY MAN.
Kenya

IT IS BY GOING AND COMING THAT THE
BIRD BUILDS ITS NEST.
Ghana

BOWING DOWN
TO SOMEONE
DOES NOT MAKE
YOU A SHORT
MAN.

Nigeria

THE POISON THAT KILLS A DOG HAS LOST ITS SCENT.

Kenya

IF YOU GO INTO A FOREST TO LOOK FOR A PERFECT STICK, YOU WILL COME OUT EMPTY HANDED.

Liberia

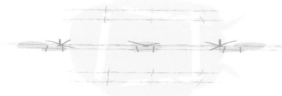

THE MONKEY ON A TREE THAT EATS WITH BOTH HANDS WILL FALL EASILY.

Sierra Leone

67

IF YOU DO NOT KNOW WHERE YOU ARE
GOING, ANY ROAD WILL TAKE YOU THERE.
South Africa

IF YOU TELL A FOOL A PROVERB, HE WILL
ASK YOU TO EXPLAIN IT.
Zambia

FOLLOW THE RIVER AND YOU WILL REACH
THE SEA.
Ghana

A HUNGRY LION WILL MAKE FRIENDS WITH A HYENA.

Botswana

THOUGH YOU WASH YOUR CLOTHES WITH HOT WATER, YOU STILL HAVE TO DRY THEM IN THE SUN.
Cameroon

WHEN THE BUSH IS ON FIRE, GRASSHOPPERS HAVE NO CHANCE TO BID EACH OTHER GOODBYE.
Kenya

IT IS SURVIVAL NOT BRAVERY THAT MAKES A MAN CLIMB A THORNY TREE.
Uganda

HOWEVER TALL
A TREE MAY BE,
IT CAN NEVER
PREVENT THE
SUN FROM
SHINING.
Nigeria

71

IF YOU WANT
YOUR DINNER
DONE, DON'T
UPSET THE COOK.
Ethiopia

CHANGING THE POT DOES NOT
IMPROVE THE TASTE OF THE FOOD
COOKING IN IT.
Ethiopia

A DOG CANNOT BITE AND BARK AT THE
SAME TIME.
Nigeria

THE WATER THAT YOU WILL DRINK
FROM THE RIVER WILL NOT FLOW
PAST YOU.

Nigeria

THE YOUNG GOAT THAT RUSHES
WILDLY TO EAT LEAVES WILL ONE-
DAY SWALLOW PRICKLY
CATERPILLARS.

Nigeria

MAKE SOME MONEY BUT DON'T LET MONEY MAKE YOU.

Tanzania

WHEN THE HEN GETS DRUNK, IT FORGETS THAT THE HAWK EXISTS.

Botswana

AN ELEPHANT DOES NOT SEE THE TICKS ON HIS OWN BODY BUT THOSE ON OTHER ELEPHANTS.
Botswana

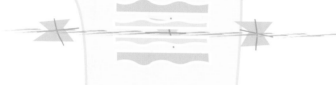

THE SMALLEST BEAST IN THE BUSH IS KING IN HIS OWN HOME.
Cameroon

DON'T CRY UNDER THE RAIN FOR YOUR TEARS WILL NOT BE SEEN.

A LAZY MAN BUILDS A HOUSE ONLY WITH HIS MOUTH.

Ghana

IGNORANCE MAKES THE RAT CHALLENGE THE CAT TO A FIGHT

Kenya

YOU CANNOT CLIMB TWO TREES AT THE SAME TIME JUST BECAUSE YOU HAVE TWO LEGS.

Kenya

78

NOT EVEN A MAD MAN HAS A LOW
OPINION OF HIMSELF.

Kenya

A WISE MAN FOLLOWS THE ADVICE OF
HIS NEIGHBOURS BUT A FOOL TRUST
HIS OWN ILLUSIONS.

Mozambique

HE WHO IS ABLE TO RUN FROM HIS
OWN SHADOW CAN ONLY
COMMUNICATE WITH THE DEAD.

Namibia

NO ONE BARGAINS FOR YAMS THAT ARE STILL IN THE SOIL.
Nigeria

A CHICKEN FEELS SAFE AT AN EAGLE'S FUNERAL
Sierra Leone

A FISH WEEPS BUT YOU DO NOT SEE ITS TEARS BECAUSE OF THE WATER THAT SURROUNDS IT.
Sierra Leone

THE MAN WITH A BIG
NOSE THINKS EVERYONE

IF YOU DO NOT SEE ANYONE LOOKING
AT YOU, DON'T CONCLUDE THAT YOU
ARE NOT BEING SEEN.
Uganda

THE LAZY MAN BLAMES HIS POOR
HARVEST ON WITCHCRAFT.
Uganda

DRUMS PLAYED IN THE NEXT VILLAGE
SOMETIMES SOUND CLEARER THAN
DRUMS PLAYED IN YOUR VILLAGE.
Zambia

IT IS NO USE OVER-FEEDING A PIG
JUST BEFORE SLAUGHTERING IT
BECAUSE YOU WANT TO EAT GOOD
PORK MEAT.
Zimbabwe

YOU SHOULD NOT TRUST A MAN WHO SAYS THAT THE HIPPOPOTAMUS IS NOT AN UGLY ANIMAL.

Gambia

IT IS AN ILLNESS THAT CAN BE CURED,
DEATH CANNOT BE CURED.
Guinea

HOWEVER HIGH YOUR SHOULDERS
GROW, THEY CAN NEVER ATTAIN THE
SAME HEIGHT AS YOUR HEAD.
Ghana

84

PEACE IS COSTLY BUT IT IS WELL WORTH
ITS PRICE.
Kenya

IF A LEOPARD SELLS GOAT MEAT, FEW
PEOPLE WILL BUY IT.
Kenya

WHERE THERE IS
NOTHING TO LOSE,
THERE IS NOTHING
TO FEAR.

Sudan

TO GET RID OF ANGER FIRST WEED
OUT THE BITTER ROOTS.
Zambia

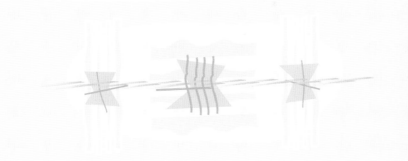

NO ONE KNOWS WHAT GOES ON
BEHIND CLOSED DOORS.
Zimbabwe

THE STRENGTH OF THE SOLDIER ANTS
LIES IN THEIR NUMBER
Nigeria

THE FIRST CAMEL PULLS THE CARAVAN
BUT IT IS THE LAST THAT GETS THE
BEATING,
Sudan

IF YOU WANT TO KNOW HOW THE
HAND IS RELATED TO THE MOUTH,
SERVE YOURSELF A DELICIOUS MEAL.
Sudan

IF YOU ARE RIDING ON AN
ELEPHANT, DON'T FORGET THAT
THERE MAY BE SLIPPERY DEW ON
THE GROUND.
Malawi

IF A FISH REFUSES TO OPEN ITS
MOUTH, IT DOESN'T GET CAUGHT.
TOGO

YOU SHOULD NOT
BEAT YOUR
CHEST WITH
SOMEONE ELSE'
HANDS.

Cameroon

A MAN HUNTING AN ELEPHANT DOES
NOT STOP TO THROW STONES AT
BIRDS.
Cameroon

YOU DON'T THROW STONES AT A
FRUITLESS TREE.
Cameroon

IT IS NOT POSSIBLE FOR ONE FOOT TO
CERATE A FOOTPATH.
Cameroon

A MONKEY THAT HOLDS THE BRANCH
OF A TREE WITH BOTH HANDS DOES
NOT EASILY FALL.
Cameroon

IF YOU LOOK INTO AN EMPTY BOTTLE
WITH TWO EYES, YOU ARE BOUND TO
SEE WHAT IT CONTAINS.
Guinea

IT IS BETTER TO FLEE DANGER AND BE
LAUGHED AT THAN TO FACE DANGER
AND BE MOURNED.
Ghana

YOU DO NOT MEASURE THE DEPTH OF
A RIVER WITH BOTH LEGS.
Ghana

EVEN THE LION, THE KING OF THE
FOREST, PROTECTS HIMSELF AGAINST
FLIES.
Kenya

PEOPLE WITH GRASS SKIRTS ON
SHOULD NOT SERVE IN A FIRE BRIGADE.
Kenya

WHEN A RAT LAUGHS AT A DOG ITS
HOLE IS NEARBY.
Nigeria

DO NOT THROW INSULTS AT A
CROCODILE WHEN YOU ARE CROSSING
A RIVER.
Nigeria

HE WHO IS SURROUNDED BY ENEMIES
SHOULD LEARN TO SLEEP WITH ONE EYE
OPEN.
Nigeria

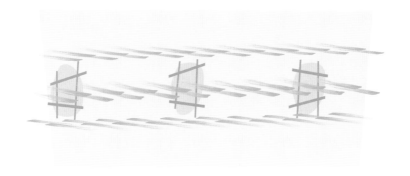

AN ANT-HILL THAT WANTS TO SURVIVE
SHOULD NOT GROW MUSHROOMS.
Sierra Leone

AN OUNCE OF EXPERIENCE IS BETTER
THAN A POUND OF BOOK KNOWLEDGE.
Sierra Leone

TICKLE THE EARTH WITH A HOE AND IT
LAUGHS WITH A RICH HARVEST.
Sudan

DON'T ATTEMPT TO HIT A RAT THAT IS
STANDING ON A CLAY POT.
Tanzania

LOOK CAREFULLY WHERE YOU ARE
GOING OR YOU MAY END UP WHERE
YOU DO NOT WANT TO BE.
Zambia

YOU CANNOT SEW A GARMENT BY
MOONLIGHT.
Zambia

IF A MAN WANTS TO BE FRIENDLY WITH
WOLVES, HE MUST FIRST SHARPEN HIS
SPEAR.
Zimbabwe

97

RUNNING WATER DOES NOT NEED A
HOLE
Gambia

A DOG WITH A BONE IN HIS MOUTH
DOES NOT BARK.
Ghana

A MAN WHO INHERITS HIS FATHER'S
WIDOW DOES NOT KNOW THAT BRIDE
PRICES ARE HIGH.
Ghana

IT IS NOT PROPER FOR THE KNEE TO
WEAR A CAP WHEN THE HEAD IS
AVAILABLE.
Ghana

IF YOU DO NOT KNOW HOW TO DANCE,
DON'T CALL A DRUMMER.
Ghana

THE INSECT THAT BITES YOU MAY BE
HIDDEN IN YOUR CLOTHES.
Ghana

THOSE WHO SPEAK TO YOU ABOUT
OTHERS WILL SPEAK TO OTHERS
ABOUT YOU.
Ghana

AN EGG HAS NO BUSINESS DANCING
ON STILTS.
Ghana

IF PROBLEMS WERE LIKE MATS TO BE
SPREAD, NO ONE WILL EVER NEED TO
COMPLAIN.
Ghana

100

YOU CAN BLAME A MAN FOR PUSHING
YOU DOWN, BUT YOU HAVE YOURSELF
TO BLAME FOR REFUSING TO GET UP.

Ghana

A CORNFIELD THAT DOES NOT GROW
WEEDS IS SURELY NOT FIT ENOUGH
TO GROW CORN.

Ghana

WHEN A HANDSHAKE EXTENDS
BEYOND THE WRIST, AND THE ELBOW,
IT IS NO LONGER A HANDSHAKE, BUT A
WRESTLING MATCH.

Kenya

YOU CAN RECOGNIZE A CHILD WHO
FAILS TO TAKE ADVICE FROM HIS
BLEEDING WOUNDS.
Lesotho

TWO GOATS WITH LOCKED HORNS
CANNOT DRINK FROM THE SAME
BUCKET.
Liberia

UNLESS YOUR BACK IS BENT, NO ONE
CAN EVER RIDE ON IT.
Malawi

TWO BIRDS TIED TOGETHER,
ALTHOUGH THEY HAVE FOUR WINGS
CANNOT FLY.
Mauritiu

IT IS THE WIND THAT TELLS THE TREES
THE KIND OF DANCE TO DANCE.
Nigeria

THE TORTOISE CANNOT MAKE ANY
PROGRESS UNTIL IT STICKS ITS NECK
OUT.

THE BULLET THAT KILLS AN ELEPHANT IS
NOT AS BIG AS THE ELEPHANT ITSELF.
Nigeria

IF A CHILD CLAIMS TO BE TOO WISE,
GIVE HIM AN ANT TO SLAUGHTER.
Nigeria

PEACE AND INJUSTICE ARE LIKE DAY
AND NIGHT: THEY CANNOT STAY
TOGETHER.
Nigeria

A DOG DOES NOT EAT THE BONE
HUNG AROUND ITS NECK.
Nigeria

YOU DO NOT INQUIRE WHO IS
RESPONSIBLE FOR YOUR FATHER'S
DEATH UNTIL YOU HAVE A SWORD IN
YOUR HAND.
Nigeria

UNTIL A ROTTEN TOOTH IS REMOVED,
ONE MUST CHEW CAREFULLY.
Nigeria

HOPE MAKES A GOOD BREAKFAST
BUT A BAD SUPPER.
Nigeria

DO NOT ARGUE WITH
A MAD MAN BECAUSE PEOPLE
WATCHING WILL NOT KNOW
WHO IS WHO.
Nigeria

YOU DO NOT HAVE TO START A
DIALOGUE WITH A COW
JUST BECAUSE YOU WANT
TO EAT BEEF.
Nigeria

A RABBIT THAT HAS ITS HOLE ON THE
FOOTPATH IS EITHER VERY BRAVE OR
IS A GOOD RUNNER.
Nigeria

IF YOU SEND SOMEONE WITH A BAG
OF SALT TO THE MARKET, DON'T SEND
A RAIN-MAKER AFTER HIM.
Nigeria

THE LAZY MAN IS DISGRUNTLED WHEN
THE COCK CROWS AT DAWN
HERALDING ANOTHER WORKING DAY.
Nigeria

THE VALUE OF PEACE IS NEVER
KNOWN UNTIL THE PEACE IS
DISTURBED.
Sierra Leone

WHEN THE HAND GRINDS
PEPPER, IT DOES SO TO THE
DISADVANTAGE OF THE
EYES AND NOSE.
Sierra Leone

WATER DOES NOT
TURN DIRTY
WITHOUT A REASON.
Sierra Leone

RESPONSIBILITY CAN ALSO CARRY
BLAME.
South Africa

THE VULTURE DOES NOT FLY OVER A
VILLAGE FOR NOTHING.
Sudan

THE MONKEY SWEATS BUT YOU DO
NOT KNOW IT BECAUSE OF THE HAIR
ON ITS BACK.
Swaziland

109

A DOCTOR WHO IS BALD TO THE NAPE
OF HIS NECK CANNOT CURE BALDNESS.
Tanzania

IT IS EASY TO STAND WITH A CROWD,
BUT IS TAKES COURAGE TO STAND-
ALONE.
Uganda

SHORT CUTS MAY CARRY MORE
TRAFFIC THAN THE MAIN ROAD.
Uganda

A COCKROACH DOES NOT NEED TO
DRESS UP TO LIVE IN A KING'S PALACE.
Uganda

NO MATTER HOW VIOLENT THE WIND MAY
BE, IT CAN NEVER FORCE THE RIVER TO
FLOW BACKWARDS.
Zimbabwe

III